EV 41

D1631809

To Emma and Silky   D.L.

To the One I love   P.V.

Published 1982 by
Methuen Children's Books Ltd,
11 New Fetter Lane, London EC4P 4EE
in association with
Walker Books, 17-19 Hanway House,
Hanway Place, London W1P 9DL

Text © 1982 David Lloyd
Illustrations © 1982 Peter Visscher

First printed 1982
Printed and bound by
L.E.G.O., Vicenza, Italy

British Library Cataloguing in Publication Data
Lloyd, David
    Air.— (The Elements; 1)
    1. Air— Juvenile literature
    I. Title II. Series
    551.5'1   QD163

    ISBN 0-416-06470-1

AIR

By DAVID LLOYD

Illustrated by PETER VISSCHER

METHUEN/WALKER BOOKS

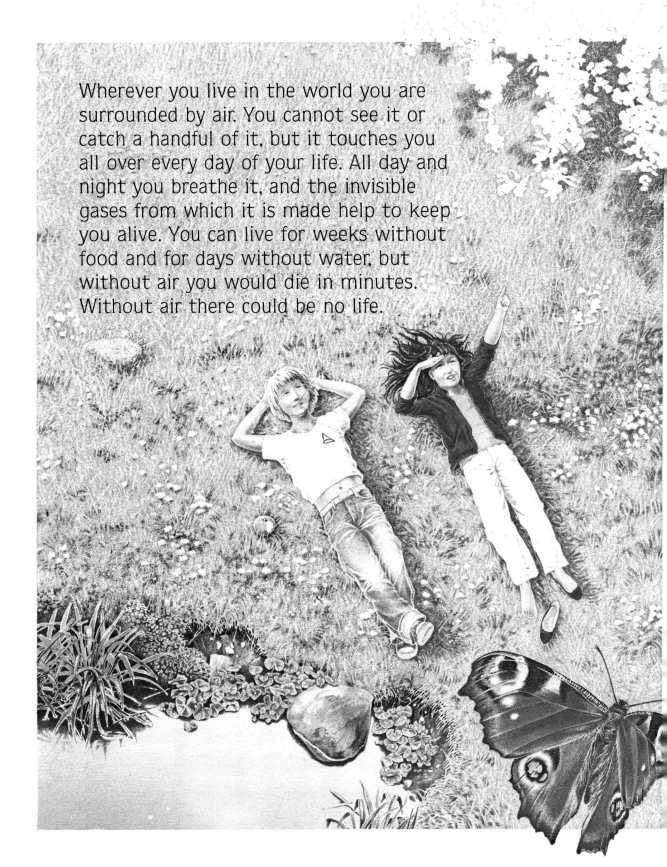

Wherever you live in the world you are surrounded by air. You cannot see it or catch a handful of it, but it touches you all over every day of your life. All day and night you breathe it, and the invisible gases from which it is made help to keep you alive. You can live for weeks without food and for days without water, but without air you would die in minutes. Without air there could be no life.

Plants are the guardians of air, because they release a gas called oxygen. Even the weeds in a city street give out oxygen. It is the oxygen in air that makes all human and animal life possible. Mixed up with the oxygen are other gases, chiefly nitrogen, with a little carbon dioxide and water vapour. Whatever the weather there is always water in the air. Clouds are just water floating in air, waiting to fall on earth as rain.

Air is always on the move, making the wind blow. Mighty rivers of air flow regularly round the world, governing the weather. Wind shows the strength of air. Trees shake and bend to let it pass, leaves and seeds are scattered by it. Sycamore seeds spin away like helicopters, dandelion seeds float away like miniature parachutes. The strength of air, as wind, helps many plants to spread from place to place.

Moving air can make the wildest winds of all. Hurricanes whirl across the land wrecking everything in their path. While lightning flickers above, a twister or tornado whips up into the sky trees, parts of houses, cars, books, chickens, horses, even people. The air forms a roaring funnel, spinning faster than any other wind on earth, sucking things up or smashing them as it races past.

For millions of years birds, bats and insects have been masters of the air. Many of a bird's bones are built like a honeycomb inside, with hollow spaces, to combine strength with lightness. Huge breast muscles power the wings. From earliest times men dreamed of flying like birds, swooping through the air with feathered wings attached to their arms. But always their bodies were too heavy and the muscles of their arms too weak.

The first men to fly successfully did so in a hot-air balloon, over Paris in 1783. Hot air always rises, obeying a natural law that applies to all gases. Heat the air in a balloon and the balloon also rises. Attach a basket underneath and you can rise with it. High above the earth, all you can hear is the creaking of the basket and faint sounds from far below. You become part of the wind, going where the wind goes.

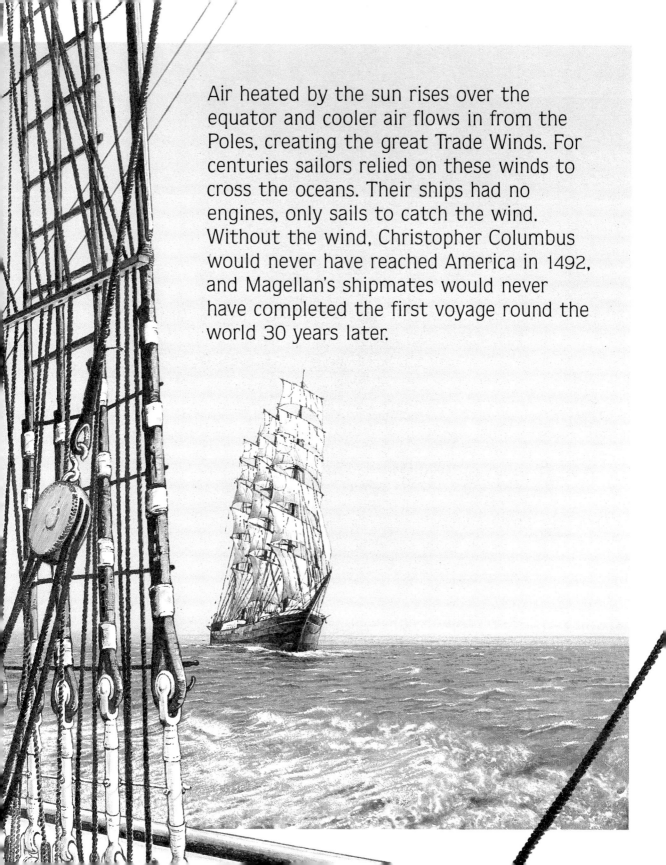

Air heated by the sun rises over the equator and cooler air flows in from the Poles, creating the great Trade Winds. For centuries sailors relied on these winds to cross the oceans. Their ships had no engines, only sails to catch the wind. Without the wind, Christopher Columbus would never have reached America in 1492, and Magellan's shipmates would never have completed the first voyage round the world 30 years later.

On land wind has also been put to many uses. Once windmills were widely used to grind corn and drain and irrigate the land. As the wind turned the sails, the machinery inside the mill was set in motion— even sawmills were powered in this way. In a few, flat, windswept places across the world, the old sails still turn, harnessing the power of air.

Today the sky is more crowded with movement than it has ever been before. In aeroplanes we have conquered the air, making the most distant places only hours away in flying time. The air has also become a place for pleasure and sport. Riding the currents on bright, coloured wings, people come close to the ancient dream of flying like a bird. Others pitch themselves into the air from aeroplanes, tumbling earthwards until they break the fall with parachutes.

Even air can get dirty. All the life and movement in big cities can burn it up, destroying its freshness. Fumes and smells can invade it, making it hard to breathe. The plants which naturally keep air fresh can be poisoned when it is too foul. Exhaust from cars and aeroplanes, smoke from chimneys— these can be the enemies of air, the things that spoil it. Air is something to look after carefully. It must be clean to be good.

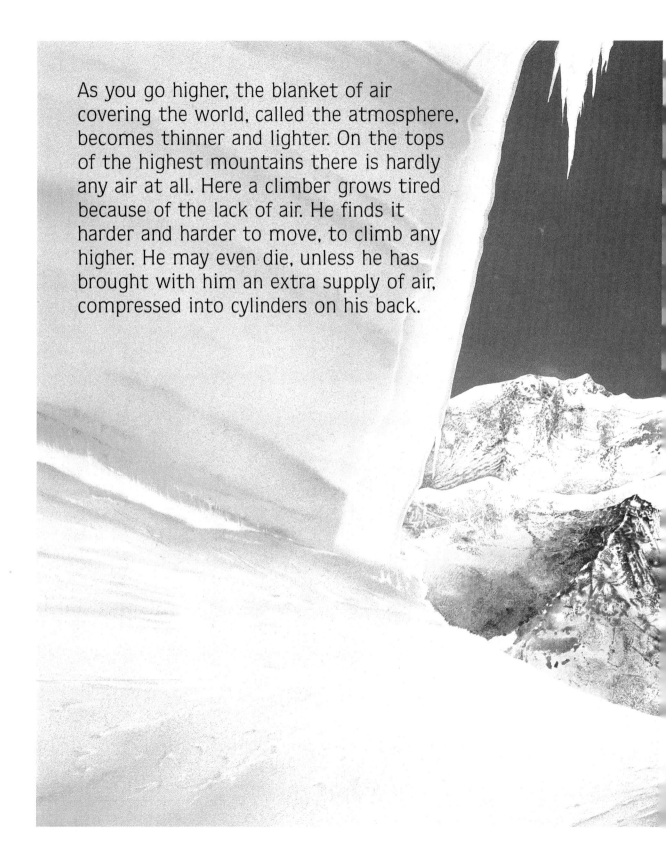

As you go higher, the blanket of air covering the world, called the atmosphere, becomes thinner and lighter. On the tops of the highest mountains there is hardly any air at all. Here a climber grows tired because of the lack of air. He finds it harder and harder to move, to climb any higher. He may even die, unless he has brought with him an extra supply of air, compressed into cylinders on his back.

Many miles up in the sky, long before you reach the moon, the atmosphere ends. There is no air in space. Men visit space, taking air with them, looking back from the silent emptiness to earth. Air swirls about the earth, making wind, making weather, making life possible. The man rolls over in space, alone in the safety of his spacesuit. Far below are all the people, all the plants, all the animals on earth. You are there too, living in the air.